James Compton Burnett

The greater diseases of the liver:

Jaundice, gall-stones, enlargements, tumours, and cancer: And their treatment

James Compton Burnett

The greater diseases of the liver:
Jaundice, gall-stones, enlargements, tumours, and cancer: And their treatment

ISBN/EAN: 9783337714857

Printed in Europe, USA, Canada, Australia, Japan

Cover: Foto ©ninafisch / pixelio.de

More available books at **www.hansebooks.com**

THE GREATER

DISEASES OF THE LIVER:

JAUNDICE, GALL-STONES,

ENLARGEMENTS, TUMOURS, AND

CANCER:

AND THEIR TREATMENT.

BY

J. COMPTON BURNETT, M. D.

" Das ist eben das wahre Geheimniss, das
Allen vor Augen
Liegt, euch ewig umgibt, aber
von Keinem gesehen."

Schiller.

PHILADELPHIA :
HAHNEMANN PUBLISHING HOUSE.
1891.

To the

Memory

OF

Rademacher

THE RESUSCITATOR OF

PARACELSIC ORGANOPATHY

THESE PAGES ARE GRATEFULLY DEDICATED

.

BY

The Author.

PREFACE.

TO those accustomed to treat diseases of the liver with remedies having an elective affinity for the organ itself, the contents of this volume must appear more or less self-evident. I refer more particularly to the practitioners of scientific therapeutics usually called homœopaths. But the practitioners of traditional medicine will find in my pages a great deal to interest them, and not a little that is new; new at least to them.

Those of my readers who have a taste for the more strictly doctrinal part of my subject, I would refer to my small work entitled "Diseases of the Spleen and their Remedies Clinically Illustrated," to which this is intended to be a companion volume.

The prevailing ignorance of good organ-remedies is lamentable. Not long since a lady came to me for a chronic liver affection of nine years' standing, and, though her physician is a man of high standing in the profession, and a doctor of medicine of the University of London, his sole treatment had consisted in giving the accursed morphia to lull the pains. He had never even tried one single good organ-remedy, and this notwithstanding the fact that patient has long been profoundly jaundiced. And this, too, is I fear, a fair sample of the everyday work of the men of light and leading in the profession.

The pain being the outcome of the disease, the treatment should have been directed to the causal complaint, and not to the effect—the pain. Had this been done the lady would, in all probability, have been cured of the fundamental disease; as it is, her disease has become formidable, and probably incurable, and she herself is a hopeless, helpless, will-less morphia eater.

It is in the hope of throwing a little light into this dismal darkness that these pages are sent to the Press.

J. COMPTON BURNETT.

5, *Holles Street,*
    Cavendish Square, W.
October 22nd, 1890.

The Greater Diseases of the Liver:

Jaundice, Gall-stones, Enlargements, Tumours, and Cancer, and their Treatment.

JAUNDICE.

IF anyone shall maintain that Jaundice is not a *greater* disease of the liver, but a minor one, I shall reply, Then such a one has never had the curious complaint. Jaundice was the indirect cause of some of my earliest efforts at independent thought in medicine; it was in this wise:—A student

B

was working with Professor H——
with the microscope while he had
a bad cold in his head—in the hot
trickling dewdrop stage—and finding that microscopizing under the
circumstances was not an easy
matter, he said to his professorial
friend, " What's good for a cold
in the head ?"

" Oh," said he, " sniff up cold
water into your nostrils—that'll
cure it quickly."

Studiosus set his microscope
aside ; went home. Once there,
forthwith sniffed cold water most
diligently into his nostrils, and
cured the said coryza there and
then. A sweet cure! as the se-
quel shewed.

The next day he had the beginning symptoms of catarrhal jaundice, and in two days the affection was well-established.

Professor H. was again consulted, and said he must give up hospital work at once, and take a holiday in the hills.

Being conversant with all the facts of the case, it occurred to me that as catarrhal jaundice was due to a catarrh of the gall-ducts, just as the coryza was a catarrh of the nose, so if we could only get at the gall-ducts as readily as at the nostrils, we might wash them out also, and thus *cure* the jaundice, as the coryza had been cured.

I have had a certain number of colds in the head to treat during the years that have since elapsed, but I have never recommended Professor H.'s plan of sniffing cold water into the nostrils, believing a catarrh of the nose to be less bad than a corresponding state of the gall-ducts. This simple narration really touches at the very foundations of *all* curing: The young man was not well; nature sought to rid his organism of something harmful to his organismic self; she set up a watery discharge from a small portion of the mucous lining of the body, near the surface and not otherwise too much functionally occupied. This hot running from the nose was really a curative expression of the organism. (The young man had been long living and working in the most foul atmosphere of dissecting rooms and hospital wards.) The cold water *stopped* it (the flux, not the disease,) and then nature fell back upon the liver, as she so often does.

Centrifugal fluxes and discharges should not be lightly stopped.

Why the flux? *Whence* the discharge? Let the questions of the why? and whence? be answered as we go along. Here I merely insist upon the elementary truth that a morbid process having a, perhaps, time-honored name, may be nevertheless no disease at all, but merely a means of cure set up by nature herself, and that there are diseases which it is disadvantageous or dangerous to cure, that is to cure in the sense in which the verb to cure is commonly used in English by the thoughtless. Of course to effect a *really* radical cure of any *primary* disease can never be other than a gain to the individual.

Case of Catarrhal Jaundice cured by *Chelidonium majus.*

A good many years since I was summoned to see a country gentle-man for sudden indisposition. It was a rather tedious railway journey, and a humble friend of the family, anxious to enlighten me, told me that the squire had the "*Yeller Janders.*" Yellow the patient was, indeed, and the colour was from jaundice! There were the usual symptoms—constipation, scanty urine of a dark yellow browny colour, and debility with depression of spirits. *Chelidonium majus* in small material doses, put matters right in a few days, leaving the patient, however, weak.

" What medicine have you been giving my husband ?"

" A new remedy."

" What's its name ?"

" *Chelidonium majus.*"

" What's the English of that ?"

" The greater Celandine."

" Then it is not by any means a *new* remedy, for it is in my old Herbal, in which it is recommended for jaundice."

And so it was: the use of the greater Celandine in jaundice has trickled down to us through the ages from the primary source of the doctrine of signatures.

Of *Chelidonium majus*, I would say that it is in this country the greatest liver medicine we have, and there is, in all conscience, no lack of hepatics. Some of my early success in practice was due to my use of *Chelidonium*.

It came about thus: I went to see an important lady for a well-known physician in the north, he being too busy to attend, but said lady strongly objected to new doctors. She took a look at me— as I subsequently learned—from a position where she herself was invisible to me, and did not like the look of me. So I was sent away with many apologies from the daughter. Her hepatalgia was easier just at the moment: she would wait till her own physician could come.

A few days later the pain in her right side became unbearable, and said physician again sent me. This time I was admitted and found her in very great pain in the hepatic region : she had had it at intervals for very many years—about thirty years, if I remember rightly. The liver was very much enlarged and the pains very acute ; there was no jaundice, the tongue mapped.

I mixed some *Chelidonium majus* and had it given pretty frequently : it eased the pain more promptly than ever the pain had been relieved before, and finally cured it altogether. Her whole life was changed. To make amends for having refused to see me on my first calling upon her she presented me with a piece of plate, and sent me subsequently very many of her suffering friends.

So *einflusserich* was this venerable dame that I feel her practical influence to this very day.

This cure, and its gratifying results to a struggling young doctor, fixed my attention a good deal upon *Chelidonium*, and upon liver affections, which are everywhere so common; and it has been my lot to relieve or cure a very large number of liver diseases—

and from this wide experience I now write.

My first real acquaintance with *Chelidonium* was from Dr. Richard Hughes's " Pharmacodynamics," a work to which I owe so much, and which I sincerely commend to all who wish to understand the actions of drugs.

I would not be too sure of my botanic knowledge, but I have an idea that *Chelidonium* is the only plant, indigenous to this country, which possesses a yellow juice. That the colour of this juice led to its use in liver diseases on the lines of the doctrine of Signatures the historically competent will hardly deny. That it has a specific affinity for the great gall-organ anyone may verify for himself if he will take a few drachms of the mother tincture in divided doses. It is kindly and gentle in its action, which action is fully set up with only a very minute dose, but inasmuch as my more intimate knowledge of it comes to me from the Rademacherians, I have generally used it in small yet material doses.

It will be interesting to give Rademacher's experience with *Chelidonium*.

He used it as an organ remedy, or in other words on the Homœopathic principle in its elementary form of specificity of seat.*

Rademacher's Use of *Chelidonium.*

Rademacher, with the charming simplicity of really great knowledge, tells us in regard to *Chelidonium*, that he had long despised it as worthless, and confessedly to his shame, for he

---

*I have entered so fully into the question of the identity of the organo-pathy of the Hohenheimians and the specificity of seat of the homœpaths, in my work entitled "Diseases of the Spleen and Their Remedies Clinically Illustrated" that I may fairly refer my readers hereto in lieu of going over the same ground again here.

remarks that it was a celebrated hepatic remedy in olden times. (See his *Erfarhrungsheillehrc,* p. 163.)

He then enters into a long dissertation upon its action and comes to the conclusion that it affects the "inner liver." He says a physician need have no great experience to know that the disease of the liver, that in its perfected form shews itself as jaundice, has endless gradations that in every-day life and in medical speech are not regarded as jaundice. Still the very slightest degree of the jaundice-affection shews itself in the urine by its pale gold colour, and in the skin, particularly in that of the face, by its more or less dirty look. And where there is but little gall in the motions and no icteric discolouration of the skin, it follows that we have in such cases to deal with not merely an obstruction to the outflow of the gall into the duodenum, but with that unknown organ by which the gall is prepared from the blood; this gall-making organ is ill, so that bile is not duly prepared at all, and therefore none can be either poured out or absorbed into the skin, or cast out by the urine. This is what Rademacher calls the " inner liver," not indeed as an anatomical expression, but as a figure of speech to convey to the mind a more or less accurate and concrete conception of the sphere of action of the *Chelidonium majus.*

This conception of the true sphere of action of *Chelidonium* is, I think, correct.

The cases cited by Radermacher are mostly " bilious fevers."

Where the gall ducts are alone implicated he considers *Nux vomica* the right remedy, Hence *Chelidonium* would be indicated in acholia as well as in jaundice when the affection is primary to the " inner liver."

Rademacher's favorite mode of

using it is the simple juice of the
plant with just as much alcohol as
will clarify and preserve it.   His
dose was at one time one scruple
of his tincture a day, but in
chronic cases of liver affections he
subsequently came down to two or
three drops a dose, given four or
five times a day.   He even came
down to one-drop doses diluted in
half-a-cupful of water, till at last
he thinks he might be accused of
copying the homœopathic posology
of " Mr. Hahnemann !"   He tells
us however ("*Erfahrungsheillehre*,"
p. 176), that he first appreciated
the curative value of small doses
from Helmont,* who roused in

---

*Opera omnia, p. 552, in the chapter
with the superscription *Butler*.

his soul the thought that *small doses of drugs might have great curative effects.*

But Rademacher confesses that he at first did not clearly perceive the importance of the small dose until he had got rid of his earlier and more gross views, and came from diligent observation to get concise views of primary organ-diseases as they really exist in nature. In a foot-note (p. 176) he protests that the small dose cannot be correctly spoken of as "homœopathic," but as being the property of Paracelsus, and refers to the eleventh chapter of the fifth book of Hohenheim's "Chirurgische Schriften," *De*

Causis et origine luis Gallicæ,
which he recommends his readers
to peruse attentively, and con-
cludes thus . . . . "wenn sie
dieses gethan, werden sie wol
nicht mehr von homöopathischen
Arzeneigaben sprechen, sondern
sie werden begreifen, dass die
Wahrheit—*unwäg und unmessbare
Arzeneigaben können, wenn das
durch Krankheit veränderte Verhält-
niss des Körpers zur Aussenwelt sich
dazu eigene, wundervolle Heilwir
kungen äussern*—mit der soge-
nannten homöopathischen Theorie
gar nicht in Berührung kommt."

In other words . . . unweighable
and unmeasurable doses of remedies can produce wonderfully

curative effects when the condition
of the body in regard to its
environment have been altered by
disease and thus rendered sus-
ceptible thereto, and thus have
nothing at all to do with the so-
called homœopathic theory.

But this only by the way, I am
writing of the Greater Diseases of
the Liver; still it is pretty evident
that Rademacher in his later days
had become conscious that his
own practice and teachings were
leading him, nilly-willy, homœo-
path-wards.

Case of Enlargement of the Liver with Jaundice cured by *Chelidonium*.

A lady of seventy, stout, and given to very little exercise, came under my observation, and on examination I found her severe and frequent right-sided pains were due to a swelled liver, which was tender in pressure. Skin and conjunctivæ subicteric, motions containing but very little bile; urine on the contrary loaded with it. She was at the seaside and this it was, she said, that had upset her liver. Tongue coated, giddy, low-spirited, pulse intermittent, insomnia, lethargic, loss of appetite, fear of death.

Chelidonium majus in small material doses resulted in complete recovery in ten days, when she returned home with a regular pulse, clear eyes and skin, and all the functions normal, and very decidedly of opinion that life, even at seventy years of age, is not at all a bad thing.

ENLARGED LIVER AND CONGESTION OF THE RIGHT LUNG, CURED BY *Chelidonium*.

A young officer in the Army was invalided home from India for liver and lung disease and came to me. I found his liver large and tender, the right lung engorged, his skin very muddy, bowels costive, and he was dreadfully depressed and weak. He was quite sure he was in consumption. The lung affection I regarded as consecutive to the engorgement of the liver, there being, in the words of Rademacher, a primary affection of the "inner" liver. *Chelidonium* in small material doses quite restored him to health in three weeks. In due course he returned to his regiment.

Case of Pronounced Jaundice Cured by *Chelidonium.*

A middle-aged gentleman, a merchant, returned from the East Indies with very severe jaundice, which had resulted in considerable emaciation. The voyage home and a stay of some duration in the north had not mended matters. He was very depressed in spirits, almost the colour of mahogany, and the urine was very scant and brown-yellow. His bowels very constipated.

How quickly and pleasantly he was cured, he even now never tires of telling his Manchester friends.

I might tell of a lady who had severe and long-lasting jaundice and who was speedily cured by *Chelidonium*, and of a notable number of other cases of liver affections cured by it, but it is needless. What I have already narrated will suffice.

I would, however, just dwell upon the fact that *Chelidonium* will very frequently cure engorgements of the right lung even when it is a concomitant of true phthisis, but it has no influence over the general phthisical state, other than what pertains to, and results from, the lower half of the right lung and liver. As an intercurrent remedy in the hepatic complications of phthisis it is capable of rendering important service.

Likewise as an intercurrent remedy in gall-stones it is useful, as is also *Myrica cerifera*, but both stand far behind *Hydrastes* in this affection.

My own conception of its true seat of action is that it affects the liver cells : Rademacher's "inner" liver.

There are numerous affections of the liver that *Chelidonium* will not touch curatively at all, and therefore it must not be regarded as a liver cure-all, which it is not.

For instance, it affects the left lobe of the liver much less than does *Carduus Mariæ*, to a consideration of which we will proceed after having first given a short account of Rademacher's use of a combination of *Chelidonium* and *Calcarea muriatica*.

RADEMACHER'S USE OF *Chelidonium* AND *Liq. Calcariæ muriat.*

Our author tells us he is convinced that there exists in nature a liver disease that can only be cured by a mixture of *Chelidonium* and *Liq Calcariæ Muriat.*

This is his formula :—

℞   Liq. Calcariæ muriat., ℥ ii.
     Tinct. Chelidonii, ℥ i.

M.

He administered fifteen drops in half-a-cupful of water five times a day. With this he cured many cases of grave fevers and hepatic affections that did not mend with either remedy by itself, but he tells us he knows of no reliable or characteristic indications for its choice.

I might add that muriatic acid once had a seemingly well-founded reputation as a liver remedy; and some still esteem it highly.

THE CURATIVE SPHERE OF *Carduus Mariæ* IN LIVER, SPLEEN, AND ABDOMINAL AFFECTIONS.

Certain remedies have very limited special spheres of influence and our power to cure diseases is largely conditioned by our knowledge of such spheres. I am increasingly impressed with the importance of knowing *where* the remedy acts by special elective affinity. As I have dealt with spleen affections by themselves, without making any special reference to *Carduus Mariæ* (the seeds are the officinal part), I will at once exemplify its action here.

Enlargement of Liver and Spleen Cured by

Carduus.

A young lady, of sixteen summers, was brought to me by her mother on the seventh of September, 1887, for severe attacks of vomiting that had lasted for three months. She was often roused rudely from her sleep in the morning with an attack of vomiting. Her constitution had been damaged by diphtheria, and eighteen months previously she had had varicella. I treated the case symptomatically with great relief to the vomiting, but the pains in the abdomen became rather worse than better.

After I had given her my old favorite *Nat. mur.* 6 she was still further improved, but there the thing still was : I had relieved the symptoms but I had not cured the real primary seat of the same. I then did what might with advantage have been done before the treatment was begun, viz.: I made a careful physical examination of the bare epigastrium and of the two hypochondria. With what result ? The note in my case book taken at the time will enlighten us . . . . "Liver and spleen both very much enlarged so that they seem almost to fill the abdomen."

Here I had to do with the severe and long-lasting vomiting which yielded partially to close symptomatic treatment but would not get quite well . . . . (Oh, how often are we in this unsatisfactory state) ; and a physical examination revealed the reason of my failure. I had treated the case with remedies that were homœpathic to the superficial symptoms, but NOT homœopathic to the cause of those symptoms; the degree of homœopathicity was not adequate though it went a long way towards it.

Here I fell back upon my Rademacherian experience with *Carduus* and gave five drops of the matrix tincture in a table spoonful

D

of water, night and morning, and this cured the enlargement both of Spleen and of Liver, and as this enlargement was the cause of the pains and vomiting, of course pains and vomiting likewise disappeared.

The only further abnormality which I could discover in the young lady after taking the *Carduus Mariæ* for about five weeks was an indurated condition of a few of the cervical glands of her left side: the side on which she had been vaccinated; *Thuja occidentalis* 30, in infrequent doses, cured these and patient has had no vomiting or any of its concomitants since. She continues well to date.

Although my own prescription of *Carduus* was from pure experience, there can be hardly any doubt that an adequate proving would shew its homœopathicity to the case, inclusive of the enlargements of liver and spleen.

Riel's proving of *Carduus* shews it to produce pathogenetically: "nausea, uneasiness, pain, vomiting, with inflation of the abdomen, &c."

The generally improved appearance of the young lady after she had been a month under the *Carduus* was very striking, and repeatedly remarked upon, by friends who were not acquainted with the circumstances of her ill-health and its treatment at all.

The *kind* of liver enlargement which *'Carduus* cures is in the transverse measurement.

By way of comparison I will now quite shortly exemplify the *kind* of enlargement of the liver which is cured by *Chelidonium ;* it will be seen that the comparison is crude and mechanical, yet withal, I submit, not without practical value.

Enlargement of the Liver in the Perpendicular Line cured by *Chelidonium*.

An independent gentleman of thirty, usually resident in Paris, came over to London to consult me in the early part of the year 1886, and that for his liver and for dyspepsia. He had twice had jaundice in previous times. His symptoms were waterbrash, indigestion, constipation, attacks of intra-abdominal chilliness; he was very dusky, his urine had a strongly urinous smell. His liver reaches almost up to the right nipple.

An ounce of the tincture brought the liver back to the normal; the dose was five drops in water, two or three times a day, and sometimes once a day. But altogether he consumed nearly an ounce.

This is the *kind* of hepatic enlargement which *Chelidonium* rights in small material doses. But it did not restore the patient to complete health; why? For the simple reason that the increase in the perpendicular measurement of the liver was only a *part* of his complaint, the other bearings of the case being foreign to my present thesis. Suffice it to say that his liver was cured by the

Chelidonium, and patient continues well in these (and now in the other) respects to the present time.

It is well to realize that an organ-remedy while capable of curing an organ-disease, and all the concomitant symptoms which *arise from* the organ-disease, nevertheless can in the nature of things *not* cure the concomitant symptoms in the patient when these symptoms stand in no nexus with such organ-disease. Thus I treated a young lady for a liver disease and gave her successively *Carduus, Chelidonium, Natrum Sulphuricum, Taraxacum.*

She had a mapped tongue and vomiting, with headaches and squinting. The liver was reduced to its right dimensions and the vomiting was cured, but the mappiness of the tongue remained, and patient did not *feel* well. But the tongue became normal after a month of *Thuja* 30. She had headaches which she herself termed bilious and the others neuralgic, and there was a third kind of headache called by another name and which seemed distinctly connected with the squinting. The bilious headaches ceased after the use of the before-mentioned hepatics; the neuralgic headaches continued till after the *Thuja*, and disappeared simultaneously with the mapped state of the tongue. The squint-headaches she still gets, and remedies like *Glonoin* and *Gelsemium* do them good.

From these considerations it is manifest that there are cases that cannot possibly be cured by one remedy and inasmuch as the symptoms form part respectively of groups of different causations, covering the totality of all the symptoms present in the patient would be a useless and fruitless task. Hence it is that Rademacherian organ-testing helps me so much in my every-day practical clinical life; for, if I cure an organ with its *Appropiatum Paracelsi*, and certain symptoms go while others remain I am enabled slowly to unravel the most complex groups of symptoms and finally find a simile or even the simillimum of the ground-evil.

The adage *Naturam morborum ostendunt curationes* also comes in here as an auxiliary. With me it is an axiom to relieve uncomfortable or dangerous organ-states with simple organ-remedies as promptly as possible, leaving the more remote and deeper-going to be afterwards considered, and treated, if possible, with its pathological simillimum, or else ætiologically, say according to Hahnemann in his Coethen phase.

Carduus Mariæ IN ITS RELATION WITH LIVER AND THE SKIN.

Perhaps it would be more correct to think of the matter as twigs of the same branch. Thus in my small work on the Skin* I mention the seeming connection between the cutaneous surface of the sternum and other internal affections, notably of the left lobe of the liver therewith.

Subsequent experience has taught me that although the *Carduus* cures these cases very

---

*"Diseases of the Skin from the Organismic Standpoint."–London, 1886.

promptly and indeed brilliantly, still the cutaneous eruption is apt to recur. In support of this connection; or, perhaps, it might be wiser to say concomitancy, I there give some *Carduus* cases thus :—

THE "STERNAL PATCH."

One often meets with liver affections connected with cutaneous manifestations.

I would like particularly to refer to a patch of eruption on the skin covering the lower part of the sternum which I have several times found co-exist with heart disease and swelling of the left lobe of the liver. In my case-takings I call it the "sternal patch."

I have four such cases in my mind at this moment, the first I will narrate is that of a mayor of a large town in the north :—He had a patch of brownish eruption on the sternal portion of thorax of the size of a woman's palm; with it were associated an enlarged liver and a cardiac affection evidenced by palpitation, systolic murmur, and general uneasiness. He came to town to see me at odd intervals for about two years, and was then discharged cured. He has passed under my observation since, but though his liver gives no trouble the same cannot be said of his skin, and he has moreover *pyor-rhœa alveolaris.*

I treated him antipsorically and organopathically, the most notable benefit being derived from *Carduus Mariæ* in five drop doses of the strong tincture given three times a day.

The second I remember was a Manchester merchant, with the same kind of cutaneous patch on the sternum, and very notable heart trouble with arcus senilis as a concomitant. Here the ease and comfort brought by the *Carduus Mariæ* were very striking. Under date of January 31*st*, 1883, I find in my case book these words of the enthusiastic patient—"It had a most marvellous effect, soon made me right; the patch went away in a fortnight; had had it for years."

This gentleman has remained under my care, calling upon me at odd times when in town, and during the past two years has had besides the strong tincture of Carduus, Bellis Perennis 1, *Aurum Metallicum* 4, Vanadium 6, and Acidum Oxalicum 3^x, and some other remedies, and I consider him vastly improved, and his life—speaking commercially—worth 40 per cent. more than previously.

The third case was that of a New York merchant, who suffered from liver and had come over to Europe to consult a physician, as he seemed to get no better from the treatment of his New York advisers. I found his liver very much enlarged, and also the before-mentioned sternal patch of skin-disease. I gave him *Carduus* in like dose to the foregoing, and he came in a week declaring himself quite well. I advised him to remain awhile under observation, to see if the cure proved permanent, but he hurried out of my room in great glee, and I never saw him again.

The fourth case in which I found the sternal patch and enlarged liver, giddiness, and palpitations of the heart, was that of a London lawyer. Here the liver got well, and the heart too, together with the giddiness, but it needed a course of antipsoric treatment to finish the cure of the patch of diseased skin. I might say the same of a fifth case, an officer in the Royal Navy, where this patch co-exists with hypertrophied liver, and in which the affair has a specific air about it, probably inherited, and it may be that when Sarcognomy is better understood, and when the relations of the various cutaneous regions will be recognized as constituting the very base of medical and medicinal diagnosis, this *sternal patch* will be understood to indicate "liver and heart."

But the following CASE CURED BY *Carduus* is also instructive in

E

considering its relationship to skin and liver.

A city merchant, thirty years of age, unmarried, came to me in May, 1888, for windy dyspepsia, the probable ground-work of which proved to be an enlargement both of liver and spleen, and he had amongst other things very numerous sebaceous cysts strewn about his body, looking for all the world like the malva seeds (cases), children call cheeses.

At first I gave *Ceanothus Americanus*, believing it to be primarily a spleen affection, and then *Pulsatilla*, but they did no great good; when *Carduus*, given for a little over a month, brought the liver back to the normal and all the wee wens were gone.

The enlargement of the liver and the wens disappeared simultaneously, but the genuinely causal nature of both was neither hepatic nor cutaneous : That was scrofula. But as scrofula can only be treated in its manifestations, he who treats such manifestations successfully cures it. The general improvement under *Carduus* was most striking and lasting : patient got quite well and has since happily married.

E. Stahl speaks in his Dissertations most highly of *Carduus* in those inflammations of the chest which are accompanied by gall fevers, and it was from him that Rademacher first learned its use and never ceased to prize it, notably in blood spitting from liver and spleen engorgements. No remedy, he declares, in our whole drug store, can compare to *Carduus* when there are stitches in the side with bloody expectoration. He recommends his readers to note well where the last trace of pain is felt as it dies away, as that is likely to be the primary seat of the real disease.

Case of Jaundice in a New-born Babe, cured by *Myrica Cerifera.*

An able accoucheur attended a lady who bore a jaundiced babe; said he, " I cannot give that wee thing any medicine, so you had better send for your homœopath (meaning me), as he can give some of his 'pips'!" This was done and pilules of *Myrica Cerifera* 3$^{\times}$ (crushed into a powder and rubbed on the baby's tongue) rapidly cured him, and he at once began to put on flesh, and has thriven ever since. Before taking the *Myrica* he was very weedy, thin, and leathery-looking.

Myrica Cerifera is one of the

very valuable additions to our *materia medica* that have come to us from America. I have often used it in liver disease, notably in bad cases of jaundice, with striking success; it produces jaundice in the healthy pathogenetically, and is very searching in its action. It was the great American Samuel Thomson, the botanic practitioner, who brought it into notice. A pale green wax is obtained from its berries, and hence it is called *ceriferus*, or wax-bearing. Its powdered bark was Thomson's "canker powder," and he advised it in all discharges from the mucous surfaces, especially in leucorrhœa, dysentery, and nasal catarrh.

Dr. Leland Walker's proving, as given in " Hale's New Remedies," shews an accurate picture of severe catarrhal jaundice; we are, therefore, on indisputably scientific ground when we prescribe *Myrica* for catarrhal jaundice. No wonder that the old American botanists practised with so much success. That Thomson was a close and accurate observer may be seen from the fact that he commends it to "disengage the thick viscid secretions of the mucous membrane," for we find Walker's pathogenetic Myrica-catarrh was of the same viscid quality; he says: "throat and nasal organs filled with an offensive *tenacious* mucus."

LEPTANDRA VIRGINICA

Is another valuable contribution from America, affecting the liver, mucous membrane, lungs, and pleura. Roughly, it is the mercury of the eclectics. It has never been a favourite of mine, simply because I have not needed it, inasmuch as it closely resembles *Chelidonium* in its effects. I once saw Dr. Reginald Jones, of Birkenhead, make a brilliant cure of a severe case of right-sided pneumonia with it—its prompt, decisive, curative action was unmistakeable.

In the lazy livers of city men, I have used *Leptandrin* $3^{\times}$ in six-grain doses with great satisfaction to the patients.

SANGUINARIA CANADENSIS is, in truth, a liver medicine, but not primarily or principally so, and is too great a remedy to be mentioned only in passing.

PODOPHYLLUM PELTATUM is a great liver remedy, and has been greatly abused. Its use in "torpid liver" is not good practice, and has done much harm. Its true scientific homœopathic use is in diarrhœa from overflowing bile, with much irritation, and even inflammation of the gut. It once stood me in good stead in a case of diarrhœa that threatened to end fatally—at any rate the allopathic family adviser had informed the lady's husband that he considered the patient would not recover, as nothing would check the diarrhœa, and the lady was seemingly sinking. I was telegraphed for, and had to travel nearly 200 miles. On arriving, the family physician, although he had given the patient up as past recovery, declined to meet me because of my homœopathic creed, and this although he professed to be a friend of the family, and only lived two doors off. The stools were foul-smelling, hot, bilious, excoriating, and passed out of the anus in a constant dribble. The patient had become too weak to be raised or even adequately helped, and things had to be just left. I studied the case a short time, and finally decided upon *Podophyllum* 6. The next evening patient was convalescent, and I returned to town. The cure was complete and permanent. When the family physician had heard of my departure, he return-ed and very kindly watched the case for me, still giving my remedy. "Why," said he, " Podo-phyllum is one of our allopathic medicines, it is not a homœopathic medicine at all; they have stolen it from us."

The poor ignoramus still knows not that the *use* of the remedy, *i. e.,* the principle on which it is used, is the point at issue.

It might be asked, why would this dapper medico not meet the writer over a supposedly dying patient, and would yet accept the more humble position of merely watching the case and giving my remedy after I had departed?

It was thus: He and another doctor in the place each considered himself the first man there; and if his rival had heard that he had met a homœopathic practitioner in proper consultation, he would have been denounced for unprofessional conduct, and his status lowered in the eyes of dear Mrs. and Dr. Grundy. He declared to the family that he personally should have been delighted to have met me, but that he had to consider his own position.

Such is medical life here in England to-day. Still, for all that, *Podophyllum* 6, humanly speaking, saved the lady's life; and I, having done my duty, have therein my reward, and I thank God for the privilege.

In the debility from jaundice I have found *Picric Acid* very helpful. I have commonly used it in the third dilution.

I have found the *Brassica Murialis*, which Dr. Heath tells me should be called *Diplotaxis*

Tenuifolia, of good service in the lazy livers of relaxing climates, when patients feel as if they could scarcely crawl about from sheer goneness. It is homœopathic to such, as I know from a fragmentary proving made by myself in 1874.

GALLSTONES.

In the treatment of gallstones we have to consider the attacks of gall colic and the treatment of the stones themselves when they lie in the gall bladder giving no one any trouble. I have treated gallstones and gallstone colic a good many times with hepatics of various kinds, and have found myself best in the painful attacks with *Hydrastis Canadensis*, originally given from a suggestion of Dr. Henry Thomas. A great many remedies stand in good repute for the treatment of this almost unique complaint. I have used as much as ten-drop doses of the strong tincture of *Hydrastis*, given every half-hour in very warm water, and known it succeed in a few hours after everything had failed. In one case the patient had lain for 40 hours in terrible agony, unrelieved by any known thing. It is odd that people who have been taking *Hydrastis*, not infrequently think they have been taking Opium. After the attack of pain is over, it is best to set about curing the liver itself by a long course of homœopathically-indicated remedies, whose names are legion ; for it must be manifest that gallstones are a secondary affection, due to a previous condition either of the liver or of the gall, or of the gall bladder, or of the linings of the ducts. In some cases I have thought the whole state had started originally in catarrhal jaundice.

My own procedure I will exemplify by narrating a case in point at some length.

CASE OF GALLSTONES AND ORGANIC DISEASE OF LIVER.

A lady of fifty years of age came under my observation early in the year 1888 with a very muddy complexion, subicteric whites of the eyes. She suffered very much from acidity and also from vomiting.

She told me she had been a sufferer from her liver for many years; severe bilious headaches and dyspepsia. She had been mercurialized for her liver till all her teeth fell out, and now her digestion had given in almost completely, and she had become so thin that her appearance was

F

quite cachetic. She had got so frightened of anything bringing on her attacks of gall colic that she avoided almost every article of food.

Owing to her great emaciation and trim build I was able to make the diagnosis of gallstones from actually feeling them, a thing I am very rarely able to do myself. The region of the gall bladder was, however, so tender that a very little feeling with my hands was as much as she could bear. I treated her for close upon two years, and then she was a plump, bonny woman, enjoying her life and dining out with her friends. Her skin had become comparatively healthy looking, though not as clear as a healthy English lady's generally is.

I chose the remedies on homœopathic indications, and here and there as Rademacher would have done; and, when I the last few times examined the region of the gall bladder, I entirely failed to find any stones.

She had the following remedies seriatim, *Ignatia amara* 1[×], *Chelidonium* 1[×] and φ, *Nux vomica* 1[×], *Cholesterine* 3[×], *Hydrastis Can.* φ, *Thuja occ.* 30, *Sanguinaria Can.* φ, *Carduus Mariæ* φ, and *Bilirubin.* 5. All these remedies did their portion of the good, and were given as they were indicated.

I have rarely seen a more satisfactory cure of a difficult, almost desperate, chronic case, and quite as rarely had a patient, with a worse family history. Which remedy cured the patient? All of them.

There is a *Carduus* case that should have come in earlier on, but I had mislaid the MS., and as it is short I will add it here, and principally because it neatly exemplifies the *Carduus* action. Five years have elapsed since the patient was cured, and there has been no return of any of the symptoms, and he has continued otherwise in uninterruptedly good health.

Hypertrophy of left lobe of the Liver; Slight Hypertrophy of the Heart; Sternal Patch.

On January 27*th*, 1885, a young gentleman, twenty-one years of age, and who had long been ailing of no one seemed to know what, was sent by his father to me "to be thoroughly overhauled and put right." The overhauling disclosed slight enlargement of the heart, considerable enlargement of the left lobe of the liver, and a very prominent sternal patch. Patient complained of suffering a good deal from giddiness.

℞ *Carduus Mariæ* ◊, five drops in water night and morning.

He was discharged permanently cured in six months. During a considerable portion of the time he was taking the *Carduus*, which quite set heart and liver right, but the sternal patch I had to cure nosodically, of which . . . *une autre fois.* I often see members of this gentleman's family including his parents, and know, as I said just now, that he has continued well ever since.

We will now return to gall-stones.

An elderly lady came under my observation early in the

summer of 1888, for gallstones, characterised by frequent recurrent attacks of jaundice, colic, and vomiting, with the usual agonizing pains. She was under me a good many months—about eighteen, if I remember rightly—and then discontinued her treatment, and has since continued well. I strongly urged her to go on longer, lest there should still be present the remains of the old colic-causing stones, but to no avail. Why should I continue taking medicines when I am well?

She had in succession (and several repeatedly), *Kali Bichromicum, Carduus Mariæ, Hydrastis Canadensis, Prunus Virginiana,*

Cholesterine, Iodoformum, and finally *Ferrum Picricum* $3^{\times}$. The last-named medicine does capital service in bilious debility.

CASE OF COLIC FROM GALLSTONES.

A middle-aged gentleman brought his wife to me three years since to be treated for gallstones, and the usual attacks of colic with vomiting, that came on at odd intervals, from known and unknown causes. Patient had been long under their own doctor in the country, but to no good purpose; in fact, a chronic pain in the right side had been super-added to the before-mentioned colic attacks, and patient had lost flesh a good deal. She paid me visits once a month for many months, until she was quite well and in a thoroughly thriving condition.

However, I told the husband that I did not think the biliary calculi were really entirely gone, and that I thought it would be wise to continue with the use of gentle gall-medicines till we had sounder ground for believing that there would be no further relapses.

But patient seemed and looked in such capital health that there really seemed, from their standpoint, no reason for continuing my treatment, so my warning was not regarded.

The remedies that helped so brilliantly in this case were *Hydrastis*, *Carduus*, *Chelidonium* and *Berberis*, and two or three others which I have not noted.

It must be fully a year since I saw any of the family, but this morning I was prescribing for her brother-in-law, who told me that she is now lying in the country very ill with gallstones, and her attending physicians consider her case hopeless. So all experience goes to show that the after-treatment of gallstones should be carried on for a very long time, so as to get rid of the disease altogether. Long delay at the printers' enables me to add that after having been thus given up, this lady again placed herself under my care, and has at last completely recovered her health, *Euonymin* and *Thlaspi Bursa Pastoris* ϕ having helped most.

How the biliary calculi are dissolved I am unable to say; that they *are* eventually really and truly got rid of by dissolution I infer from the fact that the sufferers get well and remain so.

It might be asked: What is your indication for *Bursa Pastoris* in Gallstones?

Answer: When the *original* liver-ailing *started* primarily from the womb. I will refer to this again.

CHRONIC BILOUSNESS AND EMACIATION CURED BY *Chelidonium*.

A strumous gentleman, about thirty years of age, came over from Ireland to consult me with regard to loss of flesh, dyspepsia, and biliousness. He was over six feet in height, and only weighed ten stone. Hair reddish; thorax flat; pronounced venous zig-zag; digestion very weak; poor appetite; a brownish rash across the epigastrium; cannot digest vegetables.

The state of the liver led me to prescribe *Chelidonium* 1 ; five drops in water night and morning.

Under this prescription (with the same diet, occupation, and place of abode as previously), he increased five pounds in weight in thirty-two days. In six months he had reached 10-stone 12 lbs. in weight, and he long after reported to me that he had "remained in very good health, indeed." Besides being for some months under the influence of *Chelidonium,*he had inter-currently also *Badiaga* 3$^\times$ and *Psorinum* 30, each during one month.

The state of the skin caused me to interpose *Psorinum*, and some symptoms of indigestion led me to give the *Badiaga*.

But the strikingly great amelioration set in first under the sole influence of the *Chelidonium*, but this remedy did not extend its influence far enough or wide enough, and hence it had to be supplemented by the other two, but with the spheres of action of them we are here not concerned.

ENLARGEMENT OF LIVER, PRODUCING SHORTNESS OF BREATH AND PALPITATION, CURED BY *Chelidonium majus* 3×.

Some years since a retired merchant, sixty-eight years of age, consulted me for a supposed affection of his heart. He complained of obesity, fulness in the stomach, volent perspirations on moving about—so much so that he was in the habit of changing shirts during the forenoon already; feels puffy on going up a hill; loses his breath *from the stomach* on the least hurry. Has a fresh healthy look. No arcus senilis. Is very active, and takes a good deal of exercise.

After taking twenty drops of *Chelidonium maj.* $3^{\times}$ per diem for a few weeks I noted, at his dictation: " The puffiness is much better; I can walk with greater ease; I feel as if something were gone from me." That is to say, his swelled liver had gone down and there was more playroom for his lungs and heart.

He weighed 15-stone 9 lbs., and under the action of *Chelidon-ium* this came down to 15-stone 6 lbs.

He afterwards had *Chelidonium* 1, and also *Euonymin* 3$^\times$, and after 15 months' treatment he had gone down one stone in weight, and was able to go up hill and upstairs with comfort.

I saw him a year later for neuralgia, when *Silicea* 200 was followed by the disappearance of the neuralgia.

CASE OF GALL COLIC CURED BY
Myrica Cerifera 3$^\times$.

In the year 1889 a lady of some 30 odd years of age came to consult me for her liver. She seemed healthy and bright, but severe pains in her right side, pyrosis, and certain brown patches on her skin clearly implicated the liver. Patient took for a month *Chelidonium* φ with distinct benefit. She afterwards had *Ignatia amara* 1 and subsequently *Hydrastis Can.* φ, and both with some considerable benefit.

She came then to town to see me, when I again failed to find

anything to account for her dyspepsia, though the pain I could
trace clearly to the gall-bladder.

After taking *Myrica cerif.* $3^{\times}$,
five drops in a table-spoonful of
water, for some weeks, I received
a very grateful letter from her, in
which she says: "That medicine
has done me a great deal of good ;
I have lost all pain in my side,
and have had only one headache,
and no indigestion, and I walk six
miles a day."

What the exact state of the
gall-ducts was of course I could
not tell; I could not feel any
c a l c u l i; none had ever been
passed, she thought.

Although *Chelidonium* and *Hydrastis* both did much good, it was the *Myrica* that really hit the mark curatively.

When a patient gets the *right* organ-remedy it is often really astonishing how their feeling of *bien-être* is augmented: they not only *become well*, they very emphatically *feel it;* they are, as it were, aggressively well.

Of course, a good complexion means health, more or less, but the liver is very specially involved in producing a clean skin and clear complexion; and I propose by-and-bye to dilate upon this point somewhat, as I consider it important.*

CASE OF TAWNINESS OF SKIN, BRONCHIAL CATARRH, AND COUGH.

The tawny skin is met with in greatest perfection in those who have lived in hot countries; and, where this dirty-looking dinginess of the skin is not from constitutional disease, or inherited from phthisically-disposed parents* it is quite amenable to treatment. The tawny discoloration can be more or less removed. This tawniness I re-

---

*See, on this subject, my " Five Years' Experience in the New Cure of Consumption."

gard as chronic subicterism, and, indeed, the anti-icterics cure such cases beautifully. They generally take a good deal of time to be really and permanently cured, and a whole series of such remedies have to be brought into play in succession, one after the other, together with here and there an inter-current nosode; but at times they will mend quickly from one or two remedies only.

Thus at the beginning of the current year a city merchant, fifty-five years of age, came to consult me for a cough, with a bronchial catarrh. The tawniness of his skin was very marked, and this he attributed to a twenty years' residence in Africa. The cough was habitual, and worse in the evening. There are a good many crescentic cutaneous efflorescences on his chest.

Two months of *Hydrastis Canadensis* φ.

He took altogether just an ounce, in small material doses. Cured the cough; reduced the catarrh of the bronchial lining to a minimum; and very materially lessened the tawniness of his skin; many of his friends remarking upon the very striking improvement in his seemingly dirty complexion. I should have followed up with some three or four other anti-icterics, but the gentleman considered he was well enough, and would not come any more, even "to please his wife."

THE COMPLEXION OF THE SKIN IN ITS RELATION TO LIVER AFFECTIONS.

That the compexion is more or less modified in certain affections of the liver is pretty patent to all the world, and the least observant readily remarks that "So-and-so's liver cannot be right." Nevertheless, when people's skins are in an unhealthy state they commonly treat the skin, or go to a skin doctor, who is pretty sure to regard his specialty as the first, and treats the skin, generally *d'en face*, with washes and ointments and the like.

I have tried to combat this view in my " Diseases of the Skin from the Organismic Standpoint," but, I am afraid, with too little success.

The skin gets its life from within; it is fed from within from the blood, and it is from the within that a good complexion must be obtained. One cannot make an unhealthy skin healthy by any washes or ointments whatsoever.

I have preached this doctrine before and oft, but few will listen, and hence I am going to preach .

it again, so that I may at least be able to say *dixi et animam meam salvavi.*

Take a person whose skin is jaundiced. Does anyone propose to wash the yellow skin white?

And if not, why not? It were almost as rational as to try to get a good complexion from any powders and washes whatsoever, and yet the deluded apply such things daily in faith believing.

LARGE VARICOSE VEIN; ENLARGE-
MENT OF LIVER.

It might be wondered at, that I should give a case of varicosis in a work devoted to the main diseases of the liver, but, as a matter of fact, the case is so unique that I add it here lest it be lost, and because I hardly know where it would fit in better.

At the beginning of 1889, a young lady was brought to me by her mother for a large varicose vein running from her right shoulder, over the right clavicle, and across the upper half of the right side of the chest. It varied in size somewhat, and at its largest was about the size of an ordinary quill.

Being great society people this vein quite cast a shadow over their lives, it being "quite impossible, you know, to dress."

One sees the oddest things in the way of varicose veins in the lower half of the body, but not very often in the upper, as gravitation is enough to empty them when they are higher up.

All kinds of treatment had been applied, or applied to, and quite lately the vein had been treated by that wonderful cure-nothing—electricity.

I reasoned thus: Veins that dilate in that manner, steadily, slowly, increasingly, must do so from an obstruction in their pro-gression heartwards, just as the little rivulets higher up the stream must fill up when the stream is dammed up lower down.

From a rather careful physical survey of the parts involved, I found the liver very large—indeed huge, which was probably accounted for by the fact that patient had thrice had ague, or else three attacks of the same. Her skin was dirty, dingy-looking, and the portion covering the lower end of the breast bone studded with wee flat warts, and the degree of anæmia was considerable. Moreover, she had a disagreeable cough, and her sleep was not good.

An ounce of *Chelidonium* φ, spread over eleven weeks, restored the liver to its normal size, and the varicosis had almost entirely diappeared, so that patient had again taken to evening dress—respectively, undress. Her skin at the same time became clearer, and her blood of evidently better quality.

CASE OF GALLSTONES.

The wife of a well-known clergyman came under my observation on the 12*th* of June, 1889, for gallstones. Competent medical men had attended her in these attacks, and had diagnosed gallstones. Patient had turned fifty, and is the mother of many children. Her attacks began with sharp agonizing pains in the pit of the stomach, extending to the arms, and with them severe vomiting; her breath is very short; her bowels are costive, and she is a martyr to flatulent dyspepsia.

Being a rich woman, she had sought the best advice in London, but to no avail. Her physicians had stated that nothing more could be done. Her lower extremities had begun to swell, and this, coupled with loss of flesh, dyspnœa, and a very darkly icteric coloration of the skin, seemed to corroborate the given prognosis, and the more so as patient's able physicians had long tried their best with such remedies as are current in the orthodox school of medicine.

But knowing well their poverty in remedies, and in knowledge of remedies, I set about treating this lady precisely as if she had never had any medical treatment at all.

Thirteen months later, while I am actually writing these notes, she is plump, healthy looking, and touring with her husband in Scotland, and she has had no pains at all for just eleven months. Friends who have not seen her for some time are barely able to recognize her because of her changed appearance.

Her remedies were *Hydrastis Canadensis, Bryonia alba, Thuja occident., Heloninum, Strophanthus,* and intercurrently, for far-reaching constitutional effects, two common nosodes in high dilutions.

The change in this lady's disposition is rather remarkable, as from being dull, taciturn, unengaging, and almost socially uncivil, she has become bright, affable and chatty. The fact is, our brightness and chatty sunniness in our social life do verily depend much upon the liver.

Cholesterinum in Tumour of Liver.

This is obtained from gall; I believe from that of the bullock. I learned its use of the late Dr. Ameke, of Berlin, author of the

"History of Homœopathy," trans-
lated into English by (alas, also
the *late*) Dr. Alfred Drysdale,
sometime of Cannes.

Ameke claimed to have de-
rived much advantage from its use
in *cancer of the liver*. This is a
weighty statement, and is *true*. I
believe I have twice cured cancer
of the liver with it; and, in
obstinate hepatic engorgements
that, by reason of their obstinacy,
make one think interrogatively of
cancer, the effects of *Cholesterine*
are very satisfactory: at times
even striking.

I commonly use the $3^{\times}$ trit.
in six-grain doses three times a
day, but this will here and there

H

act very violently, and when this happened I have found the third centesimal trituration effective.

Sometimes one meets with cases in which there appears to be a semi-malignant affection, involving the left lobe of the liver, and what lies between it and the pylorus and the pancreas, and here *Cholesterine* $3^\times$ and *Iodoformum* $3^\times$, in four-hourly alternation, have several times rendered me sound service.

I may relate one such. Summoned 60 miles into the country late one afternoon, to a supposedly dying lady of 60 odd years of age, I found her icteric, vomiting, bathed in cold perspiration, very thin, *débile;* the pulse small and weak, and patient seemingly almost moribund. Nothing would stay on the stomach. The seat of the affection was the left lobe of the liver, extending to the left and towards the navel. That there were gallstones is probable, but, quite *outside* of the acute attack, there was a chronic affection of some kind in the region just named, evidenced by swelling and tenderness.

Kali bich. 5 relieved; *Cholesterine* 3$^\times$ and *Iodof.* 3$^\times$ cured in a month, and, the case being of long standing, the cure converted several families to the contemned pathy of Samuel Hahnemann.

But, allowing for all doubtful-
ness and vagueness in what I here
relate, *Cholesterine* is my sheet-
anchor in organic liver disease in
which the commoner hepatics—
*Chelid.,Carduus,Myrica,Kali bich.,
Merc.*, and *Diplotaxis tenuifolia*
have failed.

I do not think that *Cholesterine*
has any influence upon the "disposition" to cancer, but it acts by
reason of its elective affinity for
the seat of the disease; it effects
therefore not a cure in the Hunterian sense, inasmuch as it
only gets rid of the product of the
disease, but that is something, as
there is then a temporary cure,
which under favourable circum-

stances may become permanent, proof of which permanence of curative results I will presently adduce. In this case the cure has proved to be permanent, as now (two years since) the lady is in capital health, and on a visit to her daughter in the North of England.

Curing the Incurable—
The Insolence of Ignorance.

"Le cancer est incurable parcequ' on ne le guérit pas ordinairement; on ne peut le guérir puisqu 'il est incurable, donc quand on le guérit c'est qu'il n' existait pas."—*Duparcque.*

The saying of Duparcque which stands at the head of this, pithily puts the whole question; the thing has not changed, *c'est alors comme alors.*

This I will dwell upon very briefly now, and at the same time bear the very highest testimony to the virtues of *Cholesterine* in cancer of the liver.

On January 30*th*, 1889, an American gentleman, confessing to sixty-five years of age, and on a visit to his daughter, married to an English clergyman in the north, was accompanied to my rooms by the said daughter, so ill was he that had I thereafter heard of his immediate demise I should have been not in the very least astonished.

The note taken at the time stands thus in my case book under the above date . . . Thin, weak, débile; yellow conjunctivæ; insomnia; very nervous and ap-

prehensive. Been treated for enlarged liver and had lots of calomel
and chloral. His skin is tawny,
cachectic. There is a swelling of
the liver or of the pancreas—
probably malignant disease of the
left lobe of the liver. Always suffered from dyspepsia. Been a
great ocean traveller. "I am
very fond of salt, and eat a great
deal." Is a practical teetotaler.
Bones of the fingers very knobby.
He is a spring-and-fall ailer. Has
lost a stone weight since November. Never been ill but ailing,
and has taken much medicine:
bromides and chloral, urethran.
Very chilly. He is very ill. Urine
normal. Has had ague, and been
twice vaccinated.

I ordered him six grains of the third decimal trituration of *Cholesterinum* every four hours, and requested him to call in a few days. The married daughter demanded my candid opinion, and I said it was, in my judgment, cancer of the liver, when she informed me that that was the unanimous opinion of all their medical advisers, the most trusted of whom were quite sure the lethal end was not far off.

That would also have been my opinion had I not seen *Cholesterine* bring back hope in several desperate cases of cancer of the liver. I therefore felt warranted in stating that I thought our remedies carefully and persistently applied might yet cure him. In a few days patient returned to me in company with his daughter, and I hardly like to say what the change was, so great was the amelioration. He looked vastly improved and walked firmly, and indeed already considered himself on the high road to recovery, almost wondering what all the fuss had been about.

When Mr. D. R. had retired, his daughter very anxiously said, " What do you think, now ?" I said I had not altered my opinion; and that the improvement was due to the remedy and not natural recovery, and that the said improvement would have to be followed up with close scientific treatment which might, and indeed most likely would, result in a positive and direct art-cure. I also tried to explain that we had begun successfully and rapidly to deal with the product of the disease, and that done we could proceed to deal with the disposition thereto. I ordered patient to go on another few days with the prescription which I had given to him at first (*Cholest.*,) and then to report himself to me.

In about half an hour thereafter the daughter returned with her husband, and the latter almost flew at me in very rage. "What," said he, "do you mean to tell me

that my wife's father has cancer?"
"Yes." And that you are going
to cure him?" "Yes. I think
I shall, but I am not sure." Here-
upon he raised his voice somewhat
and repeated his questions so
offensively that I turned away
from him and he left. I have never
seen or heard of any of them
since; nor have I ever since seen
the wife's sister, Lady ——, whom
I cured in 1886 of a Thickening
of the Cardia, but Lady ——'s
cure was a truly Hunterian one,
and she has been quite well for
long. I have been so often
amazed at the insolence of ignorance that I not infrequently find
it hard to bear with equanimity.
Thus here I was positively in-

sulted, essentially because I knew more on a given point than certain others, viz., that *Cholesterine* will at any rate curatively modify some cases that seem to be hepatic carcinosis.

Still, I thank God and take comfort . . . they know not what they do.

People who are sick of some chronic disease and are given over to their fate by those who ought at least to have the courage of hopefulness, find not infrequently their greatest enemies in their nearest relations, who resent efforts at cure. These Job's comforters seem to regard determined efforts to cure their friends as

personal insults. This pheno-
menon I have observed so often
that I have wondered what the
explanation thereof might be: in
ultimate analysis it would seem
to be human vanity. *They* have
pronounced the case hopeless, and
therefore it is so and not otherwise.

Ubi morbus ibi remedium.

This idea is very old, and
clings to mankind with wonderful
tenaciousness. On this is founded
Ameke's conception which, had he
been spared would, I think, have
resulted at least in the discovery
of notable remedies for which
clinical experience would subsequently have afforded fixed indications.

Tumour of Liver of great size Cured by *Cholesterinum.*

A country squire nearing seventy years of age came under my observation in the early part of 1889 for a very large tumour clearly connected with the left lobe of the liver. Patient was so ill that he reached town with difficulty, and became so weak that it was impossible for him to return.

Orthodoxy well represented had given him up; and his profound adynamia and cachectic look warranted me in stating that I had but small hope. But he was a plucky fellow—a type of the British aristocrat (born to govern and fit therefor : because living out of doors and *not* reading books—Beaconsfield) and he was willing to obey to the letter.

I advised him to go to the Grand Hotel and quarter himself in the sunny front high up out of the dirt and din, and there abide. He did so, and a very pleasant abode that is: the sun streaming in ; the quiet; and yet the outlook upon the seething mass below, which keeps from stagnation.

A homœopath for half a century he had boundless faith in *Nux Vomica,* but I told him that

I was sure *Nux* would not cure him, and as this visibly depressed him, I said I would give him my medicine, but in alternation with it he should have his *Nux*. Hence this was given in alternation with *Cholesterine.* The tumour slowly disappeared, the liver went down to the state it had been in for forty years, *i.e.* the left lobe somewhat bulging, and patient returned to his country seat in about two months, and ever since he is not, as a rule, conscious of possessing a liver at all, though once in a way he feels a little uneasy in the hepatic region. This I know, as patient has long been worried with vesical catarrh, and for this I am now treating him, keeping all the

I

time a certain amount of attention directed to the hepatic region in case of any further explosion; for I do not imagine that the cure thus far is a truly Hunterian one.

True, the tumour is gone and may never recur, and the gentle-man has a very healthful look; but, after all, the tumour is not itself the disease, but the disease-product.

I would not be understood to maintain that a tumour which thus goes from drug action on the *ubi morbus ibi remedium* idea must necessarily recur, but that it may. But I will continue on this same subject in my next chapter.

At the time of going to press this gentleman continues well.

Amekean Treatment of Hepatic Tumours; Hepatic Cancer.

About five years ago, a gentleman of 67 or thereabouts came under my observation for a swelling under the right ribs that competent authorities had diagnosed as of a cancerous nature. It had come a good many months subsequent to an accident: a cab wheel having gone over the body at the part mentioned. He had been under a good West-end homœopathic physician who had agreed, after close examination, to the diagnosis, and declared positively to the gentleman's wife that he had no hope whatever of curing the case, and he thought it his duty to say so.

The whole thing was quite cured with remedies in about a year; the most striking, palpable result being observed after the use of *Cholesterine* in different dilutions, though numerous remedies were needed as well, notably *Carduus Mariæ*, *Chelidonium majus*, *Myrica cerifera* $3^{\times}$, *Iodium* 1, *Kali bich.* 5, and *Nat. mur.* 6 trit.

Five years have elapsed and there has been no recurrence of tumour, and during the whole of the five years the gentleman has only been away from his business for three weeks, and that was to go to the seaside last August.

A few days since I saw his wife on her own account, when she reported him "quite well."

This certainly looks like a Hunterian cure. I can now report on another and very similar case, as follows :—

ANOTHER *Cholesterinum* CASE.

Nearly six years ago, indeed a little longer, as it was early in the year 1873, I was required to treat a liver case almost exactly like the foregoing one. But patient was not much over fifty years of age then, and it arose primarily, it was thought, from adhesive peritonitis of long before. For years this gentleman, a county man, had felt the jolting in a carriage at first uncomfortable, and latterly so painful that he had got into the habit of holding his hand against the swelled part to support it and prevent its feeling the effects of the shaking.

With the sole addition of *Medorrh. C.* the treatment was as in the last case, and of about the same duration, viz., about a year, and with an equally satisfactory result: he got well, and has remained well to date, working very hard almost all the time. This I know, as he has come about four times a year to be assured that his old enemy had been, not merely scotched, but killed.

In this case I myself originally gave a bad prognosis to the gentleman's wife, and it was the *Cholesterin* that brought life and hope into the matter. It is very difficult to cure a tumid mass of any kind with one remedy: one needs Organopathy, Homœopathy, Amekeanism, and empiricism, together with theories no end, if the full extent of the possible is to be attained.

In my judgment the full range of the art-cure of disease by remedies used on scientific lines starts from the due recognition of the primary seat of the disease, and of the remedies that electively affect such primary seat. This, I take it, is the homœopathic specificity of seat. Experience teaches me that if we are to avoid false issues in treatment we must *start* with diagnosing, if possible, *where* the malady is primarily located. At any rate, I find this the *shortest* way to curing. If this be neglected we not infrequently cover and cure the symptoms, leaving the malady itself more or less untouched.

No doubt—and on this I lay some stress—when the symptoms are scientifically (*i.e.* homœopathically) covered and cured, the disease causing the symptoms is at the same time often radically cured also; but also, and not seldom, the symptoms are got rid of, but the disease remains.

It has been urged that any untrained person can treat homœopathically by mechanically covering the symptoms; and no doubt, this is, to some extent, true. But such cures are not worth much; they do not reach very far, and are only of practical value when the malady and the symptoms are convertible terms. The simillimum of the symptoms may, *or may not* be the simillimum of the malady; if of the latter, we have an ideal therapy beyond which there is nought to be desired; if of the symptoms only, we are apt to keep on curing our patients till they die.

If homœopathy is to go on advancing we must face the question of *getting behind the symptoms*, so that we may not only treat the symptoms homœopathically, but also the malady in its essence. In other words, it will not suffice to find the simillimum of the symptoms, but that being found, it will be needful to put this pertinent question : Is this symptomatic simillimum also homœopathic to the anatomical essence of the malady itself?

In the simple and well-defined forms of disease affecting an isolated organ, Paracelsic homœopathy or organopathy is a very valuable guide to cure, and helps to define the disease and to fix its cure with the *pathologic simile.*

This results from a recognition that certain organs of the body are, as it were, organisms within the organism; minor systems within the general system. They have special individualism, both as to their functions and as to their diseases. Such an organ is the liver. It can be made ill by the organism, but, in its turn, it can make the organism ill. They act and re-act upon one another. Neither can exist without the other.

Certain drugs have been discovered by man, almost in all

places and at all times, that have an elective affinity for these organs, and these drugs have some of them received names indicative of their action, hence we have head medicines, spleen medicines, liver medicines.

This small volume is intended to shew that the greater or more common Diseases of the Liver can, for the most part, be readily cured by hepatics or liver medicines.

Inasmuch as a large number of hepatics are well-known to us, our chief difficulty lies in finding out *which remedy* will cure a *given case*. How far I have succeeded in overcoming this difficulty is shewn in these pages, and where I fail, others, beginning where I leave off, may succeed.

The cure of organ-diseases by organ-remedies is often called organopathy, and this it was that very largely constituted the practice of Paracelsus, and for which he was hounded to death. His success was so great that envy and hatred arose and fiercely attacked him. There can be no doubt that Paracelsus was foully murdered by the hired servants of his fellow-practitioners; and oh! the number of medical tomtits that have thrown dirt on his memory all through the after-living generations!

For all that, his great genius flames still right above the horizon, lighting up the life-paths of such as have the power to see. It supplies light, but not eyes.

I would remind those homœopathic practitioners who throw their little handfuls of dirt at Paracelsus that it was he—Paracelsus—who planted the acorn from which the mighty oak of homœopathy has grown.

It was just as impossible for Paracelsus to work out a homœopathic equation on the purely scientific ground of drug physiology or provings as did Hahnemann, as it was impossible for the farmers in the time of Hahnemann to use the

steam plough, *i.e.* it was not there
to be used.

I have long maintained that
organopathy is elementary homœopathy—that in the very nature of
things, homœopathy necessarily
includes organopathy.

Paracelsus was an organopath,
being the founder of organopathy.
I think it most likely that he
picked up its elements and elementary principles on his travels,
applied them in practice, and
having made cures that have rarely
been equalled, he systematized it.
Personally I acknowledge my great
indebtedness to Paracelsus,(largely
through Rademacher) with all
gratitude. I am constantly and

increasingly impressed with the importance of ascertaining the exact *primary* seat of any localised malady, and I have been driven to this by certain of my failures in purely symptomatic treatment. To really and radically heal of disease, one must often dig down and find out where the *fons et origo mali* is, and to this end Paracelsic organ-testing is of the very greatest service, indeed it often leads to the most important clinical discovery. And what may the *most* important clinical discovery be? That which *nec dextrosum, nec sinistrosum* leads straight to the goal of every true physician—mastery over disease, *i.e.*, its direct art-cure.

CASE OF GALLSTONES AND ASTHMA.

It must be nearly ten years ago that a widow lady from abroad came to consult me for asthma and biliary calculi: and I will relate her case, not only because it is apposite as a cure of a liver affection, but because the lady has been more or less within my professional ken ever since, and at this present time she is in very good health, and for long has had neither Asthma nor Gallstone attacks.

Another point of interest for me lies in the fact that four well-

K

known homœopathic physicians
had treated the case during over
three years with only indifferent
success. They treated the symptoms without any physical diagnosis, and, after having prescribed
for the symptoms and temporarily
cured many of them, the patient
remained pretty much where she
was before. Had they gone
into the case they would have
found that the bronchial asthma,
retching, and vomiting had their
point de départ in the gall bladder.

No doubt this had again its
origin in the constitutional crasis
of the individual, and hence I
began the treatment with very
infrequent doses of *Psoricum* 30.

This much lessened the pain in the right side, and it greatly relieved the cough. Then during about five weeks patient was under the influence of *Chelidonium* 1, and pain and cough quite disappeared.

In a fortnight the pain starting from the gall bladder returned, and was accompanied with much retching. Patient was of opinion that the side pain had originally come from taking such quantities of phosphorus for her cough years ago. At any rate, she affirmed that she never felt pain in this region before.

There is no return of asthma since she left off the *Chelidonium.*

I next prescribed *Terebinthina* $3^{\times}$, four drops in water three times a day. The *Tereb.* rather upset her at first, and then she got better.

After this an attack of gall colic came on from exertion.

The duskiness of the skin, and the big brown patches on the forehead, led me to give *Nux*. It did much good, and under its influence patient's skin became lighter and cleaner. Then followed *Thuja* 30, and subsequently at odd intervals, according to the symptoms, *Mercurius vivus*, *Antimon. tart.* 3, *Pulsatilla* $3^{\times}$, *Cholesterine* 2, *Ipec.*, *Alnus rub.*, *Nat. Sul.* 6, and *Calc. carb.* 30.

But these were mostly for the gallstones, as there had never been any return of the asthma after the *Psoricum* followed by the *Chelidonium*, and that is more than nine years ago.

This I consider the more remarkable, as both her own mother and her own son had asthma; and an asthmatic lady, daughter and mother of individuals similarly afflicted, would hardly have a transitory or spurious kind of asthma.

RADEMACHER'S HEPATIC.

Rademacher's liver medicines are *Quassia, Chelidonium, Liquor calc. mur., Nux vom., Crocus*, and *Carduus*, though he does not reckon the last-named as solely an hepatic. These remedies have been already sufficiently considered, excepting *Crocus* and *Quassia*, and of this latter I have myself no experience, and will therefore pass it by. Of the former I will presently speak.

RADEMACHER ON THE INFLUENCE OF *Saffron* ON THE LIVER.

Crollius, in his treatise, *De signaturis internis rerum*, cites *Saffron* as a remedy for jaundice.

Rademacher had been treating liver diseases with *Carduus*, and, finding the prevailing genius of disease alter (which he recognised from the fact that *Carduus* had ceased to cure the then prevailing liver affections), he began to test afresh for the remedy, and believed he had found it in *Quassia*.

A man of sixty years of age came under his observation for a painful chest affection, with fever, cough, and bloody expectoration— (we should now call such a case pneumonia, broncho-pneumonia, or pleuro-pneumonia, probably).

The action of *Quassia* was fair, but not so pronounced and rapid as Rademacher was accustomed to, and hence he concluded that he was not dealing with a real *Quassia* liver disease.

Patient took the *Aqua quassiæ* for a week with some obvious benefit, when, tiring of its taste, *Saffron* was added to colour and mask it. Result : rapid and complete cure.

Subsequent observations shewed that the curative virtue lay in the *Saffron*, and not in the *Quassia*.

DYSENTERIA HEPATICA CURED BY *Crocus.*

Fever, colic, vomiting, rectal tenesmus, slimy, sanguineous, non-fœcal motions, easily and promptly cured with small doses of the tincture of *Saffron*, because dependent upon a primary affection of the liver curable by *Saffron*.

"In former years I should," says Rademacher, "have rushed into print in the medical journals and proclaimed *Saffron* as the greatest liver medicine extant, but since Paracelsus has broken my spectacles I see nature with my eyes alone, and it is now manifest to me that we cannot ascribe to any organ-remedy whatsoever absolute and unconditional curative power, but that the really clear and obvious revelation of the same depends upon the kind of the epidemic genius of disease that happens for the time-being to be prevailing."

Those who know their *Syden-ham* will appreciate this.

RADEMACHER'S CURE OF GALLSTONES.

Rademacher's observations are in all cases so reliable that I deem it a useful undertaking to give, in short, the gist of his experience of the medicinal cure of Gallstones.

Carduus, he maintains, is *facile princeps* in the attack; nothing equals it, he says. He was once enabled to recognise the presence of biliary calculi in the following extraordinary manner:—

An elderly man, who had formerly complained of heartburn, fulness, and regurgitation after food, was seized with violent colic, and, as all the abdominal remedies were without effect, he concluded that the abdominal affection was symptomatic of some other primarily diseased organ. He was sent for at an unusual hour to hear from the good man's wife that a bandage with a knot in it at once stopped the pain. From this he concluded that only a mechanical affection could be thus mechanically helped.

A slight and very peculiar feeling alone remained in the region of the gall bladder. Patient was treated during six months with Durand's remedy, and was thereby completely cured of his supposed stomachic affection and of his colic. He remained quite well for twelve years. Then, after this long interval, the stony guest again put in an appearance, though under another guise. He again administered Durand's remedy whereupon the troubler ceased and came no more, the patient dying long after at a great age of senile marasm.

Rademacher relates how the symptoms of pleurisy and even of pneumonia may be really those of biliary calculi, and he instances the case of the wife, or rather widow of an admiral who was cured of an attack of gallstone colic with Durand's remedy by him, and, being seemingly well, travelled to Berlin, but fell ill of the same affection which was mistaken for pleurisy, and treated as such in the old antiphlogistic fashion with venesection and plasters, and under these the seventy-year old lady died.

Rademacher cites the case as a warning to the careless or inexperienced. He then remarks that *Sulphuric acid* has the power of stirring up biliary calculi to activity.

Of the tincture of *Carduus* in the attacks of gallstone colic he recommends from 15 to 30 drops in a teacupful of water or milk five times a day.

Mixture of Oil of Turpentine and Sulphuric Æther, or Durand's Remedy.

Paracelsus says that the oil of turpentine was first discovered by the jatro-chemists, and he strongly recommends physicians to try the curative effects of the oil in diseased human organisms.

Rademacher remarks, however, that as a rule physicians are more concerned to gain over the patient-world by saying smooth things to them than with the advancement of the healing art, and hence the recommendation was not followed and fell into oblivion.

Paracelsus affirms that turpentine with the right appropriate or organ remedies is helpful in all indurations.

Those who know of turpentine only that it is good for tapeworm, and that it, combined with æther, will dissolve gallstones, know but very little of its virtues.

He thus summarises: "All we can with certainty maintain is, that the symptoms which we ascribe to the presence of biliary calculi are not merely silenced by turpentine in æther, but by its long continued use are got rid of so completely that patients remain thereafter free of their troubles for ever, or, at any rate, for many years."

He finally remained true, after many trials, to a mixture of sixteen parts of *Spirit sulph. æth.*, and one of *Ol. tereb.*

And as to dose: one must begin gently and cautiously with ten, and, in the very sensitive, with five drops of the mixture in half a cupful of water three times a day, and the dose must be slowly or rapidly increased according to the tolerance of each individual case.

At first there is often a little pain in the liver soon after the dose, lasting a few minutes. This he declares is desirable, but the dose must not be increased till this pain has not been felt for a few days. Then the urine must be watched, and as soon as the urine begins to get darker in colour (in which case the patient at the same time is apt to complain of an uncomfortable sensation in the epigastrium), the said mixture must be temporarily stopped and *Carduus* administered till the discomfort in the epigastrium has gone, and until the urine has again become clear and of the colour of light straw. And then the mixture is to be resumed, but in a small

L

dose—smaller than it was when left off, and the dose is not to be too hastily again augmented.

.

Chronic Enlargement of the Liver cured by

Podophyllum peltatum 6˟.

In the month of June of the year 1883, a widow lady came under my observation for diarrhœa. It was clearly of hepatic nature, and patient felt as if she were sinking into the earth; icy cold feet; pains in the abdomen; has piles; last year nearly had jaundice. A physical examination revealed chronic enlargement of the liver;

patient looked ill, and in very ill-health.

With an enlargement of the liver, tenderness of the hepatic region, pains in the abdomen, piles, diarrhœa, and evident *Angegriffensein* of the organism, I think the ordination of *Podophyllum pelt.* 6$^\times$ may be fairly called scientific; in fact, I maintain that the prescription was demonstrably and strictly scientific.

It cured the patient slowly— seven weeks—surely, and permanently, and not only subjectively but objectively, for her improved appearance was very pronounced.

I often wonder in this age of science that its scientific spirit so much neglects the scientific therapeutics of Samuel Hahnemann, particularly as Hahnemann has been so long dead. It cannot now make any difference to him! And faith! it makes no difference to me either.

Then why do I stand up for homœopathy so persistently if it makes no difference to me?

Why, indeed?

Only one reason.

And what might that one reason be? Shall I confess, or let the black secret die with me?

Just this: *Homœopathy is true, that's all.*

And if true, why do people sneer at it?

Fools always do sneer at what they do not understand.

———

Practice of Modern French Physicians in the Treatment of Hepatic Colic.

M. Germain Sée, in "La Médecine Moderne," Nr. 6, 1890, treats of this subject, and shews a distinct advance on the common treatment of hepatic colic.

He notes, that the *Salicylate of Sodium* is an excellent chola-gogue; in watery solution the *Salicylate of Sodium* augments the biliary secretion, and particularly the *watery part of the bile*. And further, by a singular coincidence, this remedy, besides its action as

a cholagogue, has a powerful anal-
gesic action which is of prime
importance in the attack.

He insists that in prescribing
cholagogues great care should be
taken in dissolving them in an
ample quantity of fluid.

Rademacher was clearly of the
same view, for he gave each dose
of *Carduus* in a teacupful of fluid.

M. Sée speaks also with much
satisfaction of the free use of *Olive
Oil* in biliary attacks.

He considers purgatives con-
tra-indicated. He also condemns
all substances that lessen the
biliary secretion, such as the

salts of potassium, calomel, iron, copper, morphia, atropine, and strychnine.

But as M. Sée ignores the double and opposite actions of large and small doses, we can only regard him, in practical pharmacodynamics, as a half-educated man; and this, notwithstanding his pre-eminently leading position in the practice of modern medicine . in France. But it is something to find anyone's practice addressed to the causes of the colic, rather than to silencing the pains, which are but effects, and which, being silenced, leave the morbid state of the sufferer as bad or even worse than it was before.

Remarkable Case of Jaundice of Nine Years' duration; Gallstones of Large Size.

I really finished writing this small treatise on Liver Diseases last autumn, and sent the MS. to the printers, on the day the date of which will be found at the foot of my preface. In this same preface mention is made of a case of chronic jaundice of long duration, which I then feared was hopelessly incurable. This work has been delayed at the printers until now, owing to want of time on my part, and moreover, I have latterly delayed it somewhat on purpose, and in order that I may narrate the before-mentioned case referred to in the preface, in which I reflect upon the treatment of the case followed by a distinguished representative of old-school medicine.

I always hold that adverse criticism of a co-practitioner's work should be in the abstract, because it is not in any sense a question of persons. I also hold that whosoever criticises the work of another adversely, the same is morally bound to point out a better, a more excellent way, if he knows one.

The plan followed by my predecessor in the treatment of this case was *to lull the pain* with morphia. Now, quite apart from the deteriorating influence of the drug (a question I do not propose here to discuss), it must be manifest that the pain arose from the gallstones; and the lulling influence of the morphia not only did not cure, or even tend to cure, but actually tended to prevent nature from helping herself.

The physician knew perfectly well that he only relieved the pain ; he was quite conscious that it was in no sense a cure. "The thing," said he, "is incurable; the pain is, therefore, the legitimate object of palliative treatment." And I quite agree that a physician may not stand by and see pain without taking effective measures for its relief.

But the patient's *life* comes *first*, not the pain; and therefore, here everything hinges upon the question of curability or non-curability. Assuming that the case was really and truly incurable by medical art, then, of course, the lulling of the pain by morphia was right and proper, and moreover imperatively demanded on the ground of humanity alone; and where a physician cannot cure he is at least bound to relieve pain. I therefore attach no blame to this physician personally, his error lies in his scholastic conceptions of what are the actual possibilities of drugs in the direct art-cure of disease; and in the unqestioning belief that what he and his fellow-believers in school-physic know, covers the *entire* field of the known and of the knowable, in curative medicine.

Paracelsus is ridiculed and contemned; Rademacher is almost unknown in the wider sphere of medicine. Homœopathy is not within earshot at all, *i.e.*, in the spheres that are deemed orthodox. It seems very odd, but all that is best in medicine, in so far as it relates to the art of healing is . . . *out*side!

Paracelsus is *out*side; Rademacher is *out*side; Hahnemnn is *out*side; the physician who gave morphia for the case under study is . . . *in*side.

I will now go on to the case in question by narrating that patient, a married lady, mother of a family, was brought to me by her husband with some difficulty, owing to her great weakness and loss of flesh.

I noted as follows:—Mrs. X., 38 years of age, eleven years married, mother of seven children, came under my observation on September 29, 1890. During the past three months intensely jaundiced, and is given up as past all hope of recovery.

During the past nine years her doctor has been giving her morphia to ease the pain in the right side, left side, and in the stomach, abdomen, and hypogastrium respectively. At the present time she takes about a dozen quarter-grain pills of morphia a day; she is emaciated to a painful degree. The spleen is very much hypertrophied, and extends across to the mesial line and inferiorly down to the crest of the ilium; in fact, it practically fills the left half of the abdomen. It is very tender, and the contours of the big spleen can not only be felt but readily seen, as it rises above the surface. The liver is only very moderately enlarged, about an inch and a half beyond the ribs, towards the epigastrium.

•

While I am examining her, patient appears very weak and faint, and hardly able to bear the undressing. Her eyes are lustrous, her tongue raw red. Urine is scanty; loaded with bile; bowels costive. The region of the gall-bladder and ducts very tender, but the greatest pain is in the pit of the stomach. Catamenia always scanty, and at present stopped. The motions are without bile, and moved with the very greatest difficulty. No appetite. In almost constant distress from the agonising pains at the pit of the stomach.

Patient had been twice vaccinated, and years ago had severe
ulceration of the womb, for which
she lay in bed for three months,
and during that period was six
times cauterised. The cauterisa-
tions, aided by many introvaginal
injections and much lying-up,
were followed by the disappearance
of said ulcerations.

I did not really know where to
begin at in this formidable case,
but in view of the severity of the
epigastric pain, jaundice, constipation, &c., I ordered *Hydrastis
Can.* φ, four drops in a table-
spoonful of tepid water every four
hours. This was the last day of
September, 1890.

M

October 6*th*. The urine has begun to improve; it is more watery, and not quite so full of bile; the motions more natural, but the liver is very distinctly bigger than it was six days ago. I therefore feel justified in going on with the *Hydrastis*.

13*th*.—Patient's jaundiced skin is not quite so intensely black-yellow; the pain has *altered*. There is very distinct, though not great, improvement; for the first time for very very long her period is full and free, which has much relieved her. The spleen is a trifle smaller; the tongue dry and glazed.

I find on reference that a few doses of *Thuja* 30 were given intercurrently on the 6*th* instant. Continue with both *Hydrastis* φ and the *Thuja* 30.

20*th.*—There is no longer any pain in the region of the gall-bladder; patient complains of cold shivers; liver has gone down in size while the spleen is more swelled and very painful, and patient complains very much of chilliness.

℞ *Tc. Urticæ urentis* φ, seven drops in water three times a day.

27*th.*—No " spasms"; pains in the spleen worse; the spleen is, however, softer to the feel; liver larger. To alternate *Carduus Mar.* φ with the *Urtica*, every three hours.

Nov. 3rd.—Spleen and liver both bigger, which I take to mean that they are being acted upon by the remedies, particularly as patient is not so chilly and is in less pain. Patient has never ceased to take about a dozen morphia pills every day; some days many more.

To continue with the *Carduus* and *Urtica*.

12th.—The jaundice is much worse; the pains in the region of the gall-bladder are atrocious. I try to persuade the patient to leave off the morphia, so as to give the remedies a chance, but she appeals to me not to leave her unhelped in her agony; I could not resist, and so consented to the morphia pills being continued.

We had made a little progress in the case, but not much, and I therefore made a further and very careful survey of the ætiological history of the case, and came to the conclusion that the whole thing was of *uterine* ORIGIN.

As I have had a good deal of clinical experience of *Bursa pastoris*, tending to shew that it is a remedy specifically affecting the womb in like manner as *Chelidonium* does the liver, I at once determined to test for the right *appropriatum uteri*, as I conceive Paracelsus or Rademacher might have done.

I reasoned from the clinical
data taken in historic sequence
that the primary affection years
ago was uterine, and the hepatic
affection consecutive thereto, and
starting therefrom. I saw clearly
that the old ulcerated condition
was at the bottom of it, or rather
that was as far back as I could get
for the present. For although
the *cause* of the ulcers was presum-
ably the *fons et origo mali*, yet the
real disease *at present* to be grappled
with was the jaundice, the gallstones, and the colic.

In this case getting rid of the
primary constitutional cause would
not necessarily have mended matters, therefore I started with *Bursa*

pastoris φ, five drops in warm water every four hours.

That was on the 12*th*, and by the 17*th* there was a very extraordinary change come over the face of the case; indeed, it was at first blush almost incredible. There was much less jaundice, the liver had gone down in size almost to normality, and the spleen was fully an inch smaller. Moreover, there was no pain in the liver at all.

My inkling that the start of the disease of the biliary apparatus was in the womb being thus confirmed, indeed, rendered certain, I continued with the *Bursa* as before.

Nov. 24*th*.—Although there has been no further spasms, there has not been any further progress; patient does not sleep so well; the liver has again begun to enlarge, and there is no further diminution in the size of the spleen. Still, I did not feel justified in leaving off the *Bursa*, and hence I alternated it with *Chelidonium* φ.

December.—Patient was very ill, and everybody gave her up, excepting myself. I did not see my way out of the wood, but still I hold that the physician who gives up a case before the patient dies is on a par with the soldier who runs away from the enemy. So here, though I was absolutely alone in

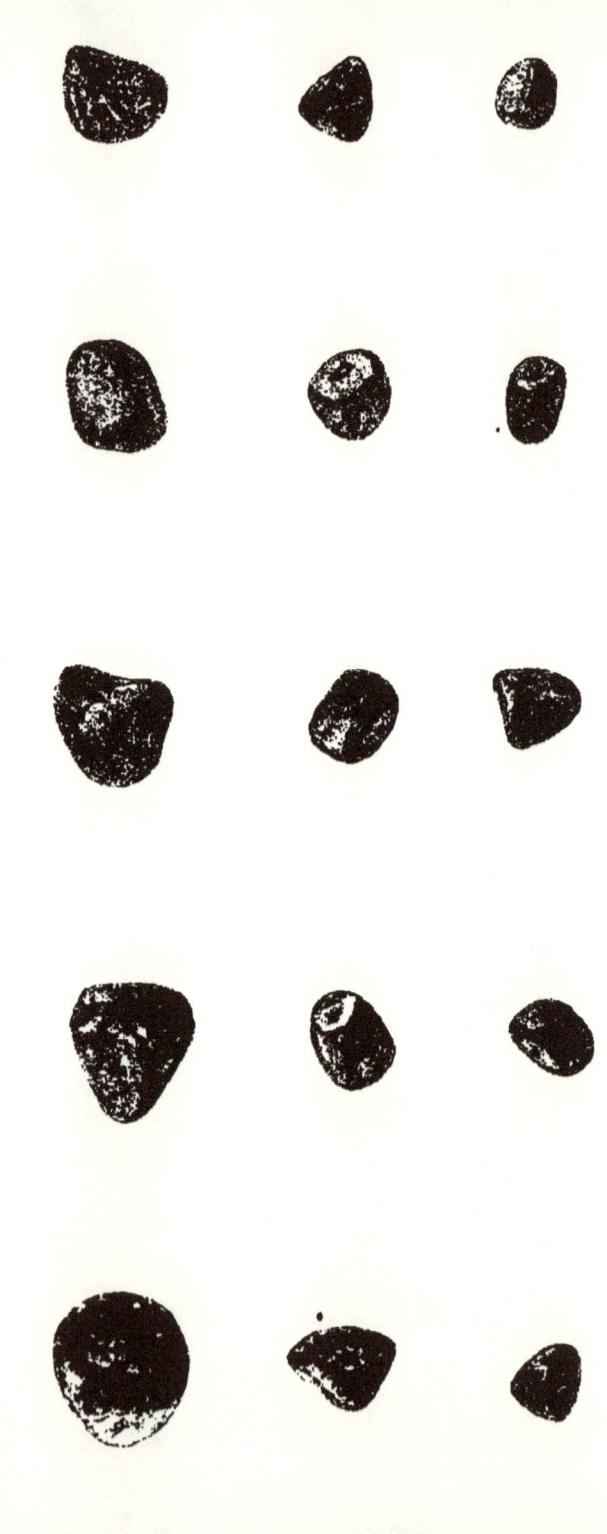

my view, I refused to surrender. The bowels had ceased to act; there was more jaundice again, and patient could no longer rise from her bed.

I then gave *Euonymin* $3^{\times}$, six grains every two hours, just as a liver remedy. Under very great agony patient in the course of a week or two passed a handful of gallstones by the bowels, and her jaundice was gone!

A number of the largest were obtained from the stools, and on account of the great interest of the case I now present my readers with a photogravure of them, taken by Sprague, of London, and which gives them in their natural size.

I have shewn these biliary calculi to certain medical friends, and amongst them to Dr. Robert T. Cooper, of London, as a curiosity.

I should explain that these biliary calculi were very much . larger than here represented when they were first passed, but their outer layers were friable, and were washed, picked, and rubbed off before the calculi were brought to me; it is really only the hard kernels of the calculi which are given in this photogravure.

Notwithstanding the disappearance of the jaundice, and the passage of the gallstones as just described, patient had got very low, and the spleen did not seem to be any better subjectively, and not much smaller, and there was no period.

Here I gave *Ceanothus Am.* 1, five drops in water four times a day.

15*th.*—Patient has had severe rigors, seemingly caused by the *Ceanothus*, which is therefore discontinued. She has no appetite, and the menstruation has not appeared.

To have *Pulsatilla* 1, three drops in water every three hours.

20*th.*—Liver nearly normal; has just menstruated; the spleen has gone down a little; the entire abdomen very tender all over; has again had an awful attack of gall-stone colic, and passed a number of stones, one very large. There is still bile in the urine.

To have *Bursa pastoris* φ, and *Nux Vom.* 1.

29*th.*—Another attack of colic; a further passage of biliary calculi —three large ones; patient is low and weak, and prefers death to so much pain. It is to be remembered that large numbers of morphia pills are being taken all this time. To relieve the effects of the passage of the calculi, and the almost general feeling of bruisedness and tenderness, I ordered *Bellis perennis* φ, eight drops in water every four hours.

1891, Jan. 12*th.*—Great general improvement from the use of the *Bellis perennis*, but her liver and spleen are more swelled and greatly distress her.

R *Trit.* 3[×] *Cholesterin.* Six grains dry on the tongue every four hours.

19*th.*—Spleen and liver seem larger than ever. No jaundice, however. No menses.

Five drops of *Pulsatilla* φ three times a day.

26*th.*—Has normally menstruated; liver smaller; spleen very
tender.

℞ *Bursa pastoris* ⚬. Five drops
in a tablespoonful of water three
times a day.

Feb. 3*rd.*—Has passed some
more calculi; region of gall duct
very tender; no jaundice; urine
normal; is gaining flesh; the
spleen is still very large.

℞ *Tr. Ceanothus Americanus* 1.
Five drops in water every four
hours.

13*th.*—There is further improvement; she feels better; is beginning to go about like other people;

has passed one gallstone of small size, and a number of lumps of "sooty stuff." Feels that this medicine has done her much good. *Rep.*

23*rd.*—The spleen has gone down about one inch and three-quarters; has menstruated again normally; is increasing in weight. *Rep.*

March 16*th.*—By letter I am informed that the spleen is not so well; and that there is a good deal of pain in the right side again.

℞ *Trit.* 3$^{\times}$ *Leptandrin.* Six grains dry on the tongue, three times a day.

31*st.*—No improvement from the *Leptandrin*, and generally not so well, though the jaundice is entirely a thing of the past, and she is now of a very clear white complexion, and getting no longer to appear to be particularly thin.

℞ *Bellis perennis* ⚲ and *Bursa pastoris* in alternation.

April 15*th.*—Liver, spleen, and womb are described as " all blown out;" much pain in the region of the gall bladder.

℞ *Puls.* and *Bryonia.*

May 4*th.*—Patient is doing well; liver normal, or nearly so; spleen now only reaches halfway down to the crest of the ilium, and is well defined. *Patient has now the old symptoms of ulceration of the os uteri—the forcible healing up of which started the whole thing years ago!*

And here I think I may resume, and conclude this already too long narration.

We see in this case the importance of Paracelsic organ-testing to find out the *point de départ* of the series of morbid phenomena; hepatics and splenics had no adequately curative action till the uterine medicine (*Bursa pastoris*) had touched the place of origin of the liver affection, and as soon as

N

this was done (see Notes under date November 17*th*, 1890) immediate improvement began !

We have now cured the jaundice; the gallstones have been got rid of through the natural ways; the liver is well, and patient is going about her business; and our interest in the case IN THIS TREATISE on "The Greater Diseases of the Liver" is at an end.

THREE MONTHS LATER.

August 10*th*, 1891.—Having this day seen and carefully examined this patient I am enabled to say that she is in excellent health, plump and pleasing, and equal to and performing the usual duties of an English housewife with a large family.

INDEX.

O

EXAMINER PUBLISHING HOUSE, LANCASTER, PA.